AF073396

No part of this publication may be reproduced or transmitted in any form or by any means, electronic or mechanical, including photocopying, recording or any information storage and retrieval system, or for the source of ideas without written permission from the publisher.

Bee Three Publishing is an imprint of Books By Boxer
Published by
Books By Boxer, Leeds, LS13 4BS, UK
Books by Boxer (EU), Dublin, D02 P593, IRELAND
Boxer Gifts LLC, 955 Sawtooth Oak Cir, VA 22802, USA
© Books By Boxer 2024
All Rights Reserved
MADE IN CHINA
ISBN: 9781915410412

This book is produced from responsibly sourced paper to ensure forest management

DOGS ARE JUST LIKE SANTA; THEIR MOTIVE IS ALSO TO SPREAD LOVE

MAY YOUR DAYS BE
SNUGGLY AND BRIGHT

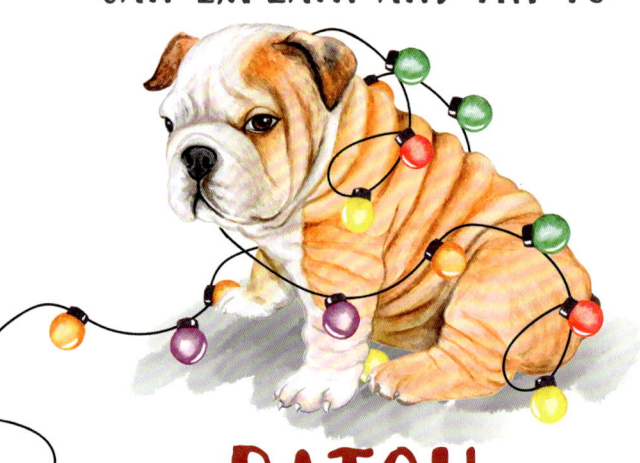

DEAR SANTA, IT WASN'T ME!

"LOVE IS A FOUR LEGGED WORD."

−UNKNOWN

PUPPY'S FUR-ST CHRISTMAS!

"So GOOD NEWS, I SAW A DOG TODAY."

– BUDDY THE ELF

OFFICIAL GIFT SNIFFER!

SENDING YOU
PUGS
AND
KISSES

MISTLETOE WISHES

AND
PUPPY DOG
KISSES!

EVEN THE GRINCH HAD A DOG. IF YOU DON'T LIKE DOGS, IT'S TIME FOR A LITTLE HOLIDAY SOUL-SEARCHING

MERRY CHRISTMAS

FROM RUDOLPH THE RED-NOSED RETRIEVER!

CHRISTMAS IS CANCELED

I TOLD SANTA YOU WERE GOOD AND HE'S STILL LAUGHING

Furry Christmas wishes and...

Wet-nosed kisses!

ALL I WANT FUR CHRISTMAS

IS A WARM LAP, EXTRA TREATS, AND LOTS OF SNUGGLES!

BARKING AROUND

THE CHRISTMAS TREE!

DIG THE YARD WITH BONES AND CHEW TOYS!

WHAT DID THE CHRISTMAS TREE SAY TO THE DOG?

YOU'RE BARKING UP THE WRONG TREE!

THE PRESENT OPENED ITSELF...
REALLY!

WISHING YOU A
PAWSOME CHRISTMAS

NOT ON MY WATCH, SANTA!

JINGLE BALLS, JINGLE BALLS, THROW THEM FAR AWAY!

"'Twas the night before Christmas, when all through the house, not a creature was stirring, not even a mouse."

—Clement Clarke Moore, A Visit from St. Nicholas

HEY SANTA PAWS

I PROMISE I TRIED TO BE GOOD!

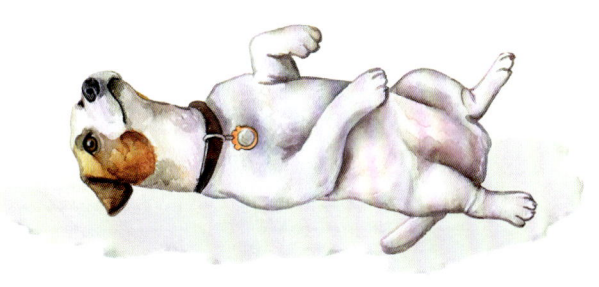

PEACE, LOVE, AND BELLY RUBS

PAW-MISE ME

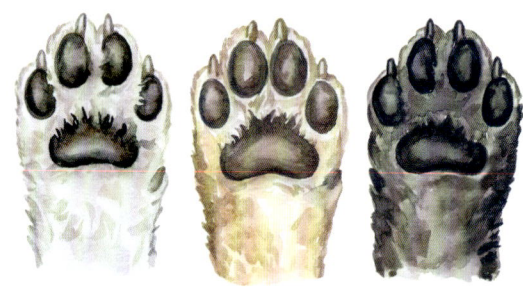

YOU'LL HAVE A
MERRY CHRISTMAS!

THERE'S A TREE IN THE LIVING ROOM...
CAN I PEE ON IT?

WE SHIH TZU A MERRY CHRISTMAS!

REINDEER ARE JUST
DOGS WITH ANTLERS!

BARKING ALL THE WAY TO THE NORTH POLE!

MY FOUR-LEGGED FRIEND IS THE...

GREATEST GIFT OF ALL!

WHAT DO YOU GET IF YOU CROSS A SNOWMAN AND A DOG?

FROSTBITE!

WHAT DID THE PUPPY SAY TO THE FRUITCAKE?

OH, CHRISTMAS TREAT, OH CHRISTMAS TREAT

"A DOG IS THE ONLY THING ON EARTH THAT LOVES YOU MORE THAN HE LOVES HIMSELF."

 — JOSH BILLINGS

A DOG IS FOR
LIFE
NOT JUST FOR
CHRISTMAS

UNLEASH THE HOLIDAY SPIRIT

HAVE A BOW-WOW-TIFUL CHRISTMAS!

DEFINE NAUGHTY...

THE ONLY PRESENT I NEED ON CHRISTMAS MORNING!

BARK!
THE HERALD ANGELS SING!

THE BEST PART OF CHRISTMAS?

WHEN THEY DROP THE TURKEY!

"THE WORLD WOULD BE A NICER PLACE IF EVERYONE HAD THE ABILITY TO **LOVE AS UNCONDITIONALLY AS A DOG.**"

— M.K. CLINTON

MY IDEA OF DECKING THE HALLS?

UNRAVELING ALL THE WRAPPING PAPER!

SHHH...
I'M LISTENING TO SEE IF THESE
PRESENTS SQUEAK!

WHY DID THE SNOWMAN TURN YELLOW?

ASK HIS DOG!

SANTA PAWS TOLD ME I'M ON THE 'NICE LIST,'

PROBABLY BECAUSE I HAVEN'T CHEWED UP HIS BOOTS... YET!

"Merry Christmas, ya filthy animal."

— Home Alone 2: Lost in New York

SNOWFLAKES ARE FOR CHASING!

WEARING ANTLERS MIGHT BE FESTIVE FOR THEM...

BUT IT'S JUST EMBARRASSING FOR ME!

"In the eyes of a dog, a **KIND WORD** and a **TASTY TREAT** can make any day feel like **CHRISTMAS.**"
— Anonymous

WISHING YOU A CHRISTMAS FILLED WITH THE WARMTH OF A DOG'S NOSE AND THE JOY OF A...

WAGGING TAIL!

WHAT DID THE DOG SAY TO THE BONE HE GOT FROM SANTA?

NICE GNAWING YOU!

CHASE YOUR TAIL IN
CHRISTMAS CHEER!

SOURCES SAY
NICE LIST
NEGOTIATIONS ARE ONGOING

LET'S BE NAUGHTY...

AND SAVE SANTA THE TRIP!

DEAR SANTA,
THE KITTEN DID IT!

UP TO
SNOW GOOD!

WHY DO DOGS HAVE THE BEST CHRISTMAS PARTIES?

THEY REALLY KNOW HOW TO RAISE THE WOOF!

DEAR SANTA, I'VE BEEN GOOD ALL YEAR. MOST OF THE TIME. ONCE. NEVER MIND.

I'LL BUY MY OWN STUFF

FESTIVE CHEER IS A
WAGGING TAIL AND FLOPPY EARS!

THE SMELL OF TURKEY IS

MALTESE-ING ME!

DECK THE HALLS WITH

BORDER COLLIES!

LET'S HAVE POODLES OF FESTIVE FUN!

I'M HAVANESE FESTIVE TREATS!

"YOU CAN'T GET THROUGH A WINTER LIKE THIS WITHOUT YOUR BUDDIES."

— SNOW BUDDIES

IT WAS THE CAT,
PINKY PAW PROMISE!

NO, I DON'T KNOW WHAT HAPPENED TO

SANTA'S COOKIES...

> "A DOG IS THE ONLY THING THAT CAN MEND A CRACK IN YOUR BROKEN HEART."
>
> — JUDY DESMOND

DACHSHUND
THROUGH THE SNOW, ON A ONE-HORSE OPEN SLEIGH!

What is a dog's favorite Christmas song?

Fleas Navidad!

WINTER MAY BE RUFF...

BUT A WAGGING TAIL MAKES

EVERYTHING BETTER!

EXCUSE ME WHILE I BE
ABSOLUTELY ADORABLE!

DECORATING MY TREE WITH TINSEL AND DOG FUR

CHESTNUTS ROASTING BY AN OPEN FIRE, PUPPY NIPPING AT YOUR TOES!

WE HOPE YOU UNLEASH ALL KINDS OF
JOY THIS SEASON!

I'M ONLY WEARING THIS FOR EXTRA TREATS...

I SAW
MOMMY KISSING
SANTA PAWS!

WINTER WOOF-DERLAND!

WHAT DO A CHRISTMAS TREE AND A DOG HAVE IN COMMON?

BARK